M000158191

"Praying … could eve… give them … and … upon … the quiet moments petitioning the Father on their behalf is one of the most loving things we could do for each other. This book will become a great guide for your prayer life."

Aaron and Jamie Ivey, (Aaron) Pastor at The Austin Stone Community Church; (Jamie) Author; Host of *The Happy Hour with Jamie Ivey*

"Any couple seeking to strengthen their prayer life will breathe a sigh of relief for the clarity, joy, and hope this guide will bring to their prayer life and marriage. I predict that, years from now, couples who use this guide will reference it when asked, 'What has been key to your healthy marriage?'"

Phillip and Jasmine Holmes, (Phillip) Chief Communications Officer, Reformed Theological Seminary; (Jasmine) Author, *Mother to Son*

"My wife Veronica and I have absolutely LOVED these *5 Things…* books. We use them as a part of our regular devotional time. The Krugers wed a wealth of scriptural knowledge to a lifetime of experience and a gift of pastoral application. You'll be blessed and changed as you use this book."

J.D. Greear, Pastor, The Summit Church, Raleigh-Durham, NC; Author, *Just Ask*

"Here is a simple, biblical, practical guide and aid to praying for your spouse, from a Christian couple that is committed to praying for one another. We thank God for Melissa and Mike, and warmly commend the book to you."

Ligon and Anne Duncan, (Ligon) Chancellor/CEO, Reformed Theological Seminary

5 THINGS TO PRAY

FOR YOUR SPOUSE

MICHAEL AND MELISSA KRUGER

thegoodbook
COMPANY

5 things to pray for your spouse
Prayers that change and strengthen your marriage
© Michael and Melissa Kruger, 2022
Series Editor: Carl Laferton

Published by:
The Good Book Company

thegoodbook.com | thegoodbook.co.uk
thegoodbook.com.au | thegoodbook.co.nz | thegoodbook.co.in

Unless indicated, all Scripture references are taken from the Holy Bible, New International Version. Copyright © 2011 Biblica, Inc.™ Used by permission.

All rights reserved. Except as may be permitted by the Copyright Act, no part of this publication may be reproduced in any form or by any means without prior permission from the publisher.

Michael Kruger and Melissa Kruger have asserted their right under the Copyright, Designs and Patents Act 1988 to be identified as authors of this work.

Published in association with the literary agency of Wolgemuth & Associates.

ISBN: 9781784986629 | Printed in India

Design by André Parker

CONTENTS

FOREWORD

BY NANCY GUTHRIE

I think most of us want to pray for our spouse. We *intend* to pray for our spouse. But we forget to pray for our spouse. Or, when we remember, our prayers can often be limited to what *we* want to see happen in their lives—the issues *we* see as urgent. And those aren't always the things that are truly most needed or most urgent.

This simple but helpful book is a tool to aid us in praying more consistently, more broadly, and more scripturally for the most important person in our lives—the one we promised to love and cherish above all others. Michael and Melissa have provided scriptural guidance and a helpful grid for asking God to do what we know he delights to do in the lives of all who are his. They're coaching us to look into God's word and turn it into prayers prayed back to him—asking him to do things like develop the fruit of the Spirit in the character of our spouse; praying that God would give them a desire to serve with joy, the grace to be content when things are hard, and a perspective that will enable them to face the future with confidence and hope.

There is a great deal each of us can do for our spouse. But there is so much that only God can do, so much that only he can develop, and so much that only he can provide. So we pray. And as we pray instead of worry, pray instead of complain, pray instead of strategize, we find that God is not only doing a work in our spouse; he's doing a work in us too. He's generating love and joy, peace and patience.

This book is helping me to set aside time to ask my Father to have his way in the life of the one I'm spending my life with, and I pray it will do the same for you.

Nancy Guthrie
Author and Bible Teacher

HOW TO USE THIS GUIDE

This guide will help you to pray for spouse in 21 different areas and situations—whether you're newlyweds or have been married for decades. There are five different things to pray for each of the 21 areas, so you can use this book in a variety of ways.

- *You can pray through a set of "five things" each day, over the course of three weeks, and then start again.*

- *You can take one of the prayer themes for the week and pray one point every day from Monday to Friday.*

- *Or you can dip in and out of it, as and when you want and need to pray for a particular aspect of family life.*

- *There's also a space on each page for you to write in the names of specific situations, concerns, or children that you intend to remember in prayer.*

Each prayer suggestion is based on a passage of the Bible, so you can be confident as you use this guide that you are praying great prayers—prayers that God wants you to pray, because they're based on his word.

5 THINGS TO PRAY

PRAYING THAT GOD WILL...

GIVE GRACE TO MY SPOUSE

1 CORINTHIANS 1 v 4-9

PRAYER POINTS:

_____

_____

_____

_____

Father, I pray you would give my spouse…

 ## GRACE TO BELIEVE

"I always thank my God for you because of his grace given you in Christ Jesus" (v 4).

It is only by God's grace that we are able to believe and trust in Christ (John 3 v 5). If your spouse is not a believer, pray that God would open their eyes to the truth of the gospel. If they are a believer, then take a moment to praise God for giving you a believing spouse. Ask God to give them a heart of thankfulness for the mercy they have received in Christ.

 ## GRACE TO SPEAK TRUTH

"You have been enriched in every way— with all kinds of speech" (v 5).

The tongue is a powerful tool that can either build up or tear down. Pray that God would give your spouse the grace to speak words of grace, truth, and peace to all those they encounter, whether it be friends, neighbors, co-workers or members of their own family.

GRACE TO UNDERSTAND

> *"… and with all knowledge" (v 5).*

We know that spiritual knowledge and understanding don't come naturally, but are gifts of God's grace. After Peter recognized Jesus as the Messiah, Jesus said to him, "This was not revealed to you by flesh and blood, but by my Father in heaven" (Matthew 16 v 17). Pray that God would grant your spouse spiritual understanding and theological discernment so they may live a life worthy of Christ.

 GRACE TO USE SPIRITUAL GIFTS

> *"You do not lack any spiritual gift…" (v 7).*

Praise God that he not only saves us by his grace but equips us by his grace to use our spiritual gifts to serve him and to bless others. Pray that God would grant spiritual gifts to your spouse in abundance, whether the gift of teaching, service, generosity, or acts of mercy. Then ask the Lord to empower your spouse to use those gifts to advance God's kingdom on earth.

 GRACE TO PERSEVERE

> *"He will also keep you firm to the end" (v 8).*

The Christian life is not easy. It's a long race in which we feel tired or even exhausted, and ready to give up. The only way we make it to the finish line is by God's grace (Hebrews 12 v 1-2). Pray that God would grant endurance and perseverance to your spouse so that they may run the Christian race with joy and faithfulness and not give in to despair and discouragement.

THINGS TO 5 PRAY

PRAYING THAT GOD WILL...

PRODUCE SPIRITUAL FRUIT

GALATIANS 5 v 22-23

PRAYER POINTS:

Father, I pray that your Spirit will bear this fruit in my spouse...

 LOVE

"But the fruit of the Spirit is love" (v 22).

Praise God that by his Spirit he gives us a new heart that bears good fruit. While our own love may run out or dry up, God's love overflows and allows us to be loving toward one another—even on difficult days when we may be disappointed or discontent in our marriage. Pray that your spouse will experience anew the love of God, and that God's love would be the source of your spouse's love for others.

 JOY AND PEACE

"... joy, peace" (v 22).

Jesus told his disciples, "In this world you will have trouble" (John 16 v 33). He also told them that he would be the source of their joy and peace in the midst of their trials. Consider what is difficult for your spouse today and ask God to give them joy in all circumstances, and a peace that transcends understanding.

FORBEARANCE, KINDNESS

"… forbearance, kindness" (v 22).

Being part of any family requires patience. Living in close quarters means we can annoy or frustrate one another. Pray that your spouse will bear with you in love. Also, pray that you would show kindness and consideration as you live with your spouse.

 ## GOODNESS, FAITHFULNESS

"… goodness, faithfulness" (v 22).

Praise God that he is the author of all that is good and he is faithful in all that he does. Each of us have many moments throughout the day when we choose whether to listen to God's ways or to go our own way. Today, pray that your spouse will follow God's word and faithfully do what is good—in their work, home, and friendships.

 ## GENTLENESS, SELF-CONTROL

"… gentleness and self-control" (v 23).

Self-control paired with gentleness is something we all hope to model. Consider today in what ways your spouse is struggling with self-control. Perhaps they are having a difficult time controlling their spending habits, limiting their screen time, or being frustrated with others. Pray that the Lord will give them self-control to do what is right, and give them gentleness in their attitude as they interact with others.

5 THINGS TO PRAY

PRAYING THAT GOD WILL...

WATCH OVER MY SPOUSE

PSALM 121

PRAYER POINTS:

_____

_____

_____

_____

Father, I pray you would watch over my spouse and…

 BE THEIR HELP

"My help comes from the LORD" (v 2).

Since we live in a fallen world, your spouse will eventually face challenges, difficulties, and discouragement. It's not a matter of if but of when. Pray that your spouse would not dwell on the problems they face but turn to the Lord who made the heavens and the earth. Take a moment to praise God for his power and strength, and be reassured that he has the ability to help your spouse in the time of need.

 KEEP THEM FROM STUMBLING

"He will not let your foot slip" (v 3).

Since life is filled with obstacles and pitfalls, it is all too easy to trip and fall while we are on the Christian journey. We are all in danger of spiritually slipping. But we serve a God who perpetually watches over us because he will "neither slumber nor sleep" (v 4). Pray that God would keep your spouse spiritually steady and firmly planted in Christ.

GIVE PROTECTION AND CARE

"The sun will not harm you by day, nor the moon by night" (v 6).

God does not promise Christians will have an easy, perfect life. It is often filled with trials and tribulations, persecutions and sufferings. But though the sun beats down, the Lord "is your shade" (v 5). Pray that he would give your spouse his presence and protection even in the midst of difficult times.

 DELIVER THEM FROM EVIL

"The LORD will keep you from all harm" (v 7).

Our fallen world is not just filled with difficult trials, but also with evil people. The psalmist is always asking God to guard him from the plots and schemes of his enemies. Pray that the Lord will protect your spouse from wicked people who may want to harm them, and vindicate them from anyone who might attack their character or wound their reputation.

 PROVIDE DAILY MERCIES

"The LORD will watch over your coming and going" (v 8).

It's easy to think that God only cares about the "big" things in our lives. So, we often forget to pray about the day-to-day things, the comings and goings. Pray through your spouse's daily routine and ask God to sustain them, encourage them, and protect them. May God remind your spouse that his mercies "are new every morning" (Lamentations 3 v 23).

5 THINGS TO PRAY

PRAYING THAT WE WILL...

LOVE EACH OTHER WELL

1 CORINTHIANS 13 v 4-6

PRAYER POINTS:

_____

_____

_____

_____

Father, I pray that your love will allow us to love one another...

 FREELY

"Love ... does not envy" (v 4).

Praise God for the love he has poured out on each of us in Christ Jesus! Yet often, when we distrust the fullness of God's love, envy creeps in and causes discontentment, quarrels, and conflicts (James 4 v 1-2). Prayerfully consider how envy might be causing disagreements in your marriage. Pray for a renewed understanding of God's love for you both so that you can love one another without envy.

 HUMBLY

"It does not boast" (v 4).

In what ways are you tempted toward pride in your marriage? Ask God to grow you in humility, considering your spouse's needs as more significant than your own. Pray that the Lord will allow you to see his blessings on your family and praise him for them, rather than boast in your own accomplishments.

3 RESPECTFULLY

"It does not dishonor others" (v 5).

It's painful to see the ways our words and actions can hurt one another. Consider how you can show honor to your spouse in your thoughts, words, and actions. If needed, confess to one another and ask God to forgive you. Ask God to grow you and your spouse in mutual respect and love for one another.

4 SELFLESSLY

"It is not proud ... it is not self-seeking" (v 4–5).

It's so easy to seek our own desires without giving thought to our spouse's needs. Pray for a self-sacrificing spirit in your marriage, asking God to make you Christ-like in your love for one another. Whether it's choosing a restaurant for dinner, making the bed, or deciding who will take out the trash, how can you love your spouse selflessly today?

5 GRACIOUSLY

"It is not easily angered, it keeps no record of wrongs" (v 5).

We often keep long lists of past hurts and wrongs committed. Old grievances awaken painful new conflicts with the words, "Remember when you did this or that." Pray that the Lord would give you both a rich love for one another that isn't easily angered and shows grace instead of keeping score.

THINGS TO 5 PRAY

PRAYING THAT WE WILL...

FOLLOW GOD'S DESIGN FOR MARRIAGE

EPHESIANS 5 v 22-33

PRAYER POINTS:

Father, I pray that in our marriage we would…

 HONOR YOUR PATTERN

"Wives, submit yourselves to your own husbands … Husbands, love your wives" (v 22, 25).

In the beginning God made both man and woman in his image—equal in value, dignity, and worth (Genesis 1 v 27). But he also made men and women different, and suited for different roles. Pray that God would give you the grace to honor the role he has given you, and pray the same for your spouse.

 LOVE SELFLESSLY

"Christ loved the church and gave himself up for her" (v 25).

Marriage is not about getting your spouse to give you what you need. Rather, it is about sacrificially loving your spouse and doing what is best for them. Christ is our perfect example: he "did not come to be served, but to serve, and to give his life as a ransom for many" (Mark 10 v 45). Pray that God would give both you and your spouse a sacrificial posture in your marriage.

GROW IN SANCTIFICATION

> "... to present her to himself as a radiant church ... holy and blameless" (v 27).

While marriage is wonderful, it can also be very difficult. But God can use those difficulties as a means to shape and change us more and more into the image of Christ. Reflect on the ways you might need to grow and change in your marriage. Where have you sinned? Where are you weak? Ask God to reveal these things to you and to empower you to change them.

 BE UNITED

> "The two will become one flesh" (v 31).

In a world filled with conflict and strife, unity is hard to come by. The same is true in marriage. If we are not careful, disagreement and conflict can set in. Ask God to give your marriage genuine unity and peace. Pray that the Lord would unite you and your spouse together in a new and special way. Also, take time to praise God for your spouse, by listing the things about your spouse for which you are thankful.

 REFLECT THE GOSPEL

> "This is a profound mystery—but I am talking about Christ and the church" (v 32).

The reason for all these prayers is that we want our marriages to look like the bond between Christ and the church. Pray that your marriage would be a faithful witness to the gospel message: that Christ gave himself for sinful people that he might love them forever.

5 THINGS TO PRAY

PRAYING THAT WE WILL...

FLEE SEXUAL IMMORALITY

1 CORINTHIANS 6 v 13-20

PRAYER POINTS:

_____

_____

_____

_____

Father, I pray that you will help us to…

 ## AVOID SEXUAL SIN

"The body … is not meant for sexual immorality" (v 13).

Praise God that we are fearfully and wonderfully made! God created sexual intimacy and it is a blessing—thank him for this gift in marriage. Pray that God would protect your marriage from all forms of sexual immorality: lustful thoughts, inappropriate emotional attachments, and adultery.

 ## HONOR THE LORD

"… but for the Lord" (v 13).

God is our Creator and our bodies are meant to honor him. Pray that the Lord would keep you from using your bodies to selfishly gratify your own desires (even in marriage) and that you would glorify him. Ask for strength to serve others as you present your bodies as living sacrifices, holy and acceptable to God (Romans 12 v 1).

3 TRUST THE LORD

"By his power God raised the Lord from the dead, and he will raise us also" (v 14).

We need the Lord's strength. The world has so many temptations—pornography, lust, and adultery seem to be everywhere. Ask God to strengthen your hearts by his resurrection power and help you walk in newness of life with regard to sexuality. Pray for his power to be at work in your lives and to give you freedom to obey his word.

4 REMEMBER OUR UNION

"But whoever is united with the Lord is one with him in spirit" (v 17).

Praise the Lord that you are united with Christ; rejoice that his righteousness freely covers all the sin of those who repent. Ask God to keep you mindful of your union with Christ, as well as your union with your spouse. Pray that this knowledge would help you to fight for sexual purity.

5 FLEE SEXUAL IMMORALITY

"Flee from sexual immorality" (v 18).

When we're in grave danger, we know we need to flee and run away. Sexual sin is particularly dangerous because it's a sin against our own body. Pray that you would be quick to flee from any form of sexual immorality. Ask God to keep your thoughts pure and your actions honorable—may you flee from sin and run in the course of his commands.

33

THINGS TO PRAY 5

PRAYING THAT WE WILL...

SERVE GOD WITH OUR GIFTS

ROMANS 12 v 3-8

PRAYER POINTS:

_____

_____

_____

_____

Father, I pray you would help us to use our gifts...

 HUMBLY

> *"Do not think of yourself more highly than you ought" (v 3).*

Gifts can so easily become a source of pride. But Paul reminds his readers that these gifts are all due to grace (v 6). So, pray that God would keep you and your spouse from pride and self-confidence and instead allow you to use your gifts with humility and "sober judgment" (v 3). Ask that your gifts would result in God's glory, not your own.

 FAITHFULLY

> *"... in accordance with the faith God has distributed to each of you" (v 3).*

It is by faith and trust that we use the gifts that God has apportioned to each of us. Sometimes God gives the gifts the church needs, not necessarily the gifts we want. Pray that the Lord would give you reassurance that your gifts are appropriate to who you are.

3 COMMUNALLY

"So in Christ we, though many, form one body" (v 5).

God does not give spiritual gifts simply to bless an individual, but for the good of the entire church as we work together. Pray that God would give you and your spouse a solid church home in which you can serve and use your gifts. Or think through the ways you're already exercising your gifts and ask God to use them to bless the overall body of Christ.

4 DIVERSELY

"We have different gifts" (v 6).

While God desires spiritual gifts to bring unity, that doesn't mean they are all the same. Pray that God would help you appreciate not only your own gifts but the goodness of other people's gifts. Take a moment to praise God for your spouse's giftedness, thanking him for the way he is using them to build his church.

5 ZEALOUSLY

"If your gift is prophesying, then prophesy … if it is serving, then serve…" (v 6-7).

It's one thing to have spiritual gifts, it's another thing to faithfully and actively use them. The tragedy is that many Christians are unaware of their gifts, or let them sit idle. Paul doesn't want us to make this mistake. Pray that God would give your spouse the energy and zeal to use their gifts, as well as the opportunities and outlets within the body of Christ to do so.

5 THINGS TO PRAY

PRAYING THAT WE WILL...

OPEN UP OUR HOME TO OTHERS

ROMANS 12 v 13-18

PRAYER POINTS:

_____

_____

_____

_____

Father, allow our home to be a place where we…

 HELP OTHERS

"Share with the Lord's people who are in need" (v 13).

Sometimes it's difficult to know what others need. Ask God to give you and your spouse wisdom. Whether someone needs a word of encouragement, a warm meal, heartfelt prayers, or financial assistance, pray that God would show you how to contribute in your church, your neighborhood, and beyond.

 SHOW HOSPITALITY

"Practice hospitality" (v 13).

Praise God that he has given you a place to call home. While it's natural to want our home to be a refuge and retreat for our family, pray that your home would also be a warm and welcoming place to invite others. May others find it a joy to sit at your table, not because the décor is perfect or the food is gourmet, but because they experience the love of Christ. Ask God to make your home a place where the lonely find community, the sorrowful find comfort, and the weary find rest.

3 REJOICE

"Rejoice with those who rejoice" (v 15).

It's a gift to have friends with whom we can laugh and rejoice. We want our homes to be places where we celebrate job promotions, weddings, babies, and birthdays with deep joy in God's blessings. Pray that your home would be full of rich community and rejoicing with others as you share your lives with them.

4 MOURN

"Mourn with those who mourn" (v 15).

There are so many difficult circumstances in this life. Friends suffer as a result of grief, divorce, job loss, physical pain, spiritual doubt, and financial distress. Pray that the Lord would make your home a place of comfort and care. Ask God to let you walk alongside loved ones and share their tears as they mourn painful circumstances.

5 LIVE IN HARMONY

"Live in harmony with one another" (v 16).

Some days it seems like everyone is at odds with everyone else. There's so much division and conflict in our world; pray that, in contrast, your home would be a place of peace. Pray that your family would live in harmony with one another and seek to live in harmony with others. Ask God to help you to be good neighbors and serve others with Christ-like love and care as you seek to "live at peace with everyone" (v 18).

THINGS TO PRAY 5

PRAYING THAT WE WILL...

HONOR GOD WITH OUR MONEY

PROVERBS

PRAYER POINTS:

_____

_____

_____

_____

Father, when it comes to money please help us to...

 GIVE FIRST TO GOD

> *"Honor the LORD with your wealth, with the firstfruits of all your crops" (3 v 9).*

One of the biggest dangers of money is that we can begin to think if we earned it, then it's ours. This is why God calls us to tithe a portion to him—it's a reminder that he, not money, is first in our lives. Take a moment to praise God for the way he has blessed you financially. Then, ask God to help you to set apart his portion first, trusting that he will provide for you.

 BE HARD WORKERS

> *"The lazy do not roast any game, but the diligent feed on the riches of the hunt" (12 v 27).*

Humans are always looking for a shortcut to financial stability. We want to get rich quick so we can relax. But God reminds us that hard work, not laziness, is what honors him. Pray that God would give you and your spouse diligence and perseverance in your work.

44

3 SAVE WISELY

"A good person leaves an inheritance for their children's children" (13 v 22).

When it comes to money, the message of our world is often spend, spend, spend—enjoy it all now. But the Christian has hope for more than just this life. So, we can save diligently and sacrificially for the good of our children. Ask the Lord to give you and your spouse financial wisdom—knowing when to save, when to spend, and how to be wise as you plan for the future.

4 BE GENEROUS TO THE POOR

"One who oppresses the poor to increase his wealth and one who gives gifts to the rich—both come to poverty" (22 v 16).

While it is not sinful to have money, God asks us not to neglect those who are in need. Ask the Lord to give you and your spouse a heart for the poor, a generous spirit, and a desire to help those around you. Pray that you would find the greatest joy in giving your money away.

5 NOT LOVE MONEY

"Do not wear yourself out to get rich; do not trust your own cleverness" (23 v 4).

"The love of money is a root of all kinds of evil" (1 Timothy 6 v 10). Consider whether you need to change or repent in this area. Ask God to keep your hearts away from the love of money and centered solely on the love of Christ.

45

5 THINGS TO PRAY

PRAYING THAT MY SPOUSE WILL...

HONOR GOD IN THEIR LABORS

COLOSSIANS 3 v 22 – 4 v 1

PRAYER POINTS:

Father, may my spouse work in way that prioritizes…

 OBEDIENCE

"Obey your earthy masters" (v 22).

Some of us have bosses who lead well and are easy to follow, while others have bosses who are difficult or discouraging to follow. Ask God to give your spouse a trusted leader and good boss to work for. But pray also that your spouse will obey the leadership of whoever God has put over them, as well as the laws of your country, insofar as they honor and glorify God.

 SINCERITY

"… with sincerity of heart and reverence for the Lord" (v 22).

Praise God for the work he has given your spouse today! While we may sometimes approach our tasks with grumbling and complaining, it is a blessing to have work to do. Pray that your spouse will work today with a heart of genuine joy and enthusiasm, and that they would be a blessing and encouragement to others. Ask God to encourage your spouse and give them thankfulness as they work.

48

3 DILIGENCE

"Work at it with all your heart" (v 23).

As we seek to honor God in our work, it overflows in our actions. Pray that your spouse will work in all aspects of their job with diligence. May they be willing to go the extra mile, work with humility, and serve others in their labors. Ask the Lord to sustain your spouse in their hard work and allow them to enjoy a Sabbath rest each week as a gift from him.

4 SERVICE

"It is the Lord Christ you are serving" (v 24).

It's tempting to work for the applause of other people—be that a customer, client, or colleague. However, our ultimate goal is to honor God in all our labors, remembering that we are working to please him. Pray that the Lord will help your spouse to remember who they are truly working for today and that their work would glorify God.

5 FAIRNESS

"Masters, provide ... what is right and fair, because you know that you also have a Master in heaven" (4 v 1).

At times in our work, we are in authority over others. Pray that your spouse would be a wise manager of all those who are under their care—treating their team with honesty, fairness, patience, and respect. Pray that they will lead in such a way that it will be a joy for others to work for them.

PRAYING THAT MY SPOUSE WILL...

SHARE THEIR FAITH WITH OTHERS

MATTHEW 28 v 18-20

PRAYER POINTS:

_____

_____

_____

_____

Father, I pray that my spouse would be an evangelist who…

 TRUSTS GOD'S SOVEREIGNTY

"All authority in heaven and on earth has been given to me" (v 18).

Sometimes people ask, "If God is sovereign, then why bother sharing your faith?" But Jesus reminds us that his divine authority is the only grounds for hope that our evangelism will be successful. Pray for your spouse's outreach, asking that they would trust that Jesus is in control. Lift up the names of their lost friends to Jesus, asking him to sovereignly open their eyes to the truth of the gospel.

 SEEKS OUT THE LOST

"Therefore go…" (v 19).

Ask God to give your spouse the diligence and courage to leave their comfort zone and reach out to the lost where they are, rather than expecting the lost to come to them. Ask that God would open up opportunities for them to share their faith wherever they might go.

FOCUSES ON DISCIPLESHIP

"Make disciples..." (v 19).

True evangelism is not just concerned with winning converts, but with producing disciples—men and women who know Jesus and want to follow him faithfully. And discipleship takes time, energy, and commitment. Pray that God would give your spouse the desire and the opportunity to invest deeply into the lives of others. Ask the Lord to lead your spouse to just the right people that God wants them to disciple.

 CARES ABOUT THE CHURCH

"Baptizing them..." (v 19).

Baptism demonstrates that a person is part of Christ's visible church. The Great Commission is ultimately about building the church; pray that your spouse's evangelistic efforts would be focused on that too. Praise Christ for his promise to build his church, knowing that the gates of hell will not prevail against it (Matthew 16 v 18).

 TEACHES THE WHOLE TRUTH

"Teaching them to obey everything I have commanded you" (v 20).

When we share the gospel with people, sometimes we are tempted to leave out the controversial parts. But Jesus reminds us that we are to teach everything he commanded. Pray for courage to speak the truth, even when it's unpopular; and for open hearts to receive that truth, even when it's difficult.

5 THINGS TO PRAY

PRAYING THAT MY SPOUSE WILL...

DELIGHT IN GOD'S WORD

PSALM 119

PRAYER POINTS:

Father, I pray that your word will give my spouse...

 DELIGHT

"I delight in your decrees" (v 16).

It can be easy to believe that delight will be found in enjoying a new TV show, restaurant, or fun evening out with your spouse. While we can enjoy these things together, there's a deeper joy to be found in God's word. Ask God to give your spouse deep delight in the word, trust in its truth, and hope in its promises.

 UNDERSTANDING

"Give me understanding, so that I may keep your law" (v 34).

Praise God that he is willing to teach us his ways! God's word is the source of all knowledge and understanding—and it's meant to be a blessing, not a burden. Prayerfully consider ways you can seek God together for wisdom from his word. Ask God to help your spouse understand and apply his word in the decisions they face today.

COMFORT

"My comfort in my suffering is this: your promise preserves my life" (v 50).

We need comfort. Whether your spouse is suffering from physical ailments, doubt, depression, financial strain, or relational hardship, pray that God's word will offer specific comfort in their situation today. Ask God to give you life-giving words of truth to encourage and comfort your spouse.

GUIDANCE

"Your word is a lamp for my feet, a light on my path" (v 105).

Sometimes the path ahead seems so unclear, and circumstances difficult to understand. While God's word may not speak to our specific situation, it does faithfully lead us. Pray that your spouse will turn to God's word for guidance today, and that the Spirt will direct their thoughts and actions and keep them from walking in opposition to God's word.

HOPE

"I have put my hope in your word" (v 147).

Thank God that he is faithful to fulfill his promises. While it may be tempting to put our hope in a better job, a bigger house, or a restful vacation, pray that your spouse would put their hope in God, not the lesser promises of this world. Pray that the Spirit would remind your spouse of God's word throughout their day, causing their heart to overflow with abiding hope.

5 THINGS TO PRAY

PRAYING THAT MY SPOUSE WILL...

BE WISE

PROVERBS 13

PRAYER POINTS:

Father, make my spouse wise with their...

 WORK

"A sluggard's appetite is never filled, but the desires of the diligent are fully satisfied" (v 4).

God cares very much about how we work. Pray that your spouse would work with energy, diligence, and perseverance for the glory of God, and that they would not succumb to the temptation to cut corners or work half-heartedly (Colossians 3 v 23). And ask God to bring much fruit from their labors.

 MONEY

"Dishonest money dwindles away, but whoever gathers money little by little makes it grow" (v 11).

People can become so obsessed with money that they will do anything to get more of it. Pray that God would help your spouse engage in financial matters with honesty, integrity, and patience. Ask him to help your spouse resist the world's temptation to love money.

3 JUDGMENT

"Good judgment wins favor, but the way of the unfaithful leads to their destruction" (v 15).

In order to navigate the many pitfalls of our world, we need wisdom to judge between right and wrong, and good and evil. Pray that your spouse would grow in their understanding of God's word so that they might make wise and godly decisions. Ask that God would protect your spouse from the paths of destruction and lead them to the path of life.

4 FRIENDSHIP

"Walk with the wise and become wise, for a companion of fools suffers harm" (v 20).

Pray that the Lord would provide for your spouse deep, meaningful, and godly friendships which will point them toward Christ. Also, ask that the Lord would protect them from bad company and from those who would lead them away from Christ.

5 PARENTING

"The one who loves their children is careful to discipline them" (v 24).

Parenting is one of the most wonderful and also most difficult tasks to which we can be called. If you have children, ask God to bless you in your parenting. In particular, ask God to help your spouse be diligent in providing loving discipline to your children, but also to do so with wisdom, gentleness, and patience.

5 THINGS TO PRAY

PRAYING THAT MY SPOUSE WILL...

BE JOYFULLY CONTENT

PHILIPPIANS 4 v 1-13

PRAYER POINTS:

Father, may my spouse find their joy in you and...

 REJOICE

"Rejoice in the Lord always. I will say it again: Rejoice!" (v 4).

Spend some time praising God for who he is and all that he has done for you in Christ. Rejoice in the Lord! Pray that your spouse will experience great joy by worshiping and rejoicing in Jesus. May the joy of the Lord be your strength.

 FIGHT ANXIETY

"Do not be anxious about anything, but in every situation, by prayer and petition, with thanksgiving, present your requests to God" (v 6).

Anxiety quickly steals our joy. What is your spouse anxious about today? Whether it is a stressful job situation, health struggle, or relational conflict, pray they would experience the peace of God guarding their minds in Christ Jesus as they turn to him in prayer.

GUARD THEIR THOUGHTS

"Whatever is true, whatever is noble, whatever is right, whatever is pure, whatever is lovely, whatever is admirable—if anything is excellent or praiseworthy—think about such things" (v 8).

It's tempting to spend our mental energy comparing ourselves to others or complaining about what we lack. Ask God to help your spouse to take every thought captive to Christ and choose to think upon what is right, true, lovely, excellent, and praiseworthy.

 LEARN CONTENTMENT

"I have learned the secret of being content in any and every situation" (v 12).

In marriage, we will experience times of plenty and times of want. Some days our lives will be full of love and laughter, while others will be filled with sadness and sorrow. Pray that your spouse will grow in contentment in every circumstance—that God would enlarge their heart for every difficulty they encounter.

 TRUST JESUS

"I can do all this through him who gives me strength" (v 13).

Contentment is impossible in our own strength. We need a source of refreshment outside of ourselves. Consider where your spouse is struggling to be content. Pray they'll learn to depend on God's strength as they seek to be content in all things.

65

5 THINGS TO PRAY

PRAYING WHEN WE ARE...

SUFFERING TRIALS

JAMES 1 v 2-4

PRAYER POINTS:

_____

_____

_____

_____

Father, in the midst of trials help my spouse…

 TRUST YOUR PURPOSES

"You face trials of many kinds" (v 2).

Since we live in a fallen, broken world, we will all meet with various trials at some point in our lives. Whatever the difficulty, God has a purpose. Pray that your spouse would recognize that trials are not random, unexpected, or a sign that God is against them. Ask that God would reassure your spouse that he has a good purpose for the trials we endure.

 HAVE JOY

"Consider it pure joy" (v 2).

Even in the midst of trials it is possible to have real joy. Not because we pretend the trials don't really exist, but because we put our hope and trust in the good God who is behind the trials. Ask the Lord to give your spouse supernatural joy as they endure this season of suffering. Pray that the Lord would give your spouse a heart of praise and thankfulness for all the blessings in their life.

INCREASE IN FAITH

"... because you know that the testing of your faith produces perseverance" (v 3).

In order for athletes to grow stronger or run faster, they have to push their bodies to extreme limits. They have to test themselves. So it is with our faith. Pray that the Lord would use these trials to increase the faith of your spouse so that they trust God more deeply and rely on him more fully, knowing that God really loves and cares for them.

 BE STEADFAST

"Let perseverance finish its work..." (v 4).

There's one thing everyone wants to do in the middle of trials: give up. Like a runner who is exhausted, we just want to stop. Pray that God would use these trials to produce an extra degree of steadfastness in your spouse—that they may learn to persevere in the midst of difficulty. Ask the Lord to use that extra endurance to produce spiritual fruit in other parts of their life.

 GROW IN MATURITY

"... so that you may be mature and complete, not lacking anything" (v 4).

God's ultimate goal for his people is that they would be more like Christ. Ask the Lord to use these trials to shape and mold your spouse so that they may be a more mature Christian, ready for whatever may come their way.

5 THINGS TO PRAY

PRAYING WHEN WE ARE...

EXPERIENCING CHANGE, UNCERTAINTY, OR FEAR

JOSHUA 1 v 8-9

PRAYER POINTS:

Father, when we are experiencing change, uncertainty, or fear, let us...

 MEDITATE ON GOD'S WORD

> *"Keep this Book of the Law always on your lips; meditate on it day and night" (v 8).*

Change is difficult. We tend to find security and comfort in routine. Whether you are moving cities, changing careers, or bringing home a new baby, change can be unsettling and difficult in marriage. Pray that God's word will be an anchor and comfort for your family in the midst of uncertainty and fear.

 OBEY GOD'S WORD

> *"... so that you may be careful to do everything written in it" (v 8).*

Fear can lead to bad choices. When we are concerned about finances, stressed because of work, or fearful of relationship conflict, we may think that obedience to God is too costly. Pray that in the midst of fears, you and your spouse will trust God and do what is right, even when it may come at a cost.

PROSPER

"Then you will be prosperous and successful" (v 8).

So many of our fears revolve around our future. Will we ever pay off this debt? Will we be able to have children? Will our parents be ok? Prayerfully entrust your concerns to God, asking that he will do what is best. Pray that he will bless you with what you need for spiritual health—no more, and no less (Proverbs 30 v 8–9).

 BE STRONG AND COURAGEOUS

"Be strong and courageous. Do not be afraid; do not be discouraged" (v 9).

There's a lot to be concerned about in our world—it's tempting to cover our eyes and shrink back in fear. However, we can prayerfully and courageously go to battle against our fears, asking the Lord to strengthen us for whatever we may endure. What are you facing today as a couple that is causing anxiety or uncertainty? Pray that together you will have strength and courage as you trust the Lord with your circumstances.

 KNOW YOUR PRESENCE

"The LORD your God will be with you wherever you go" (v 9).

Christians are not promised a life of ease, but we are promised that we are never alone in our trials. Praise God! Pray that you and your spouse will experience the security of God's presence in the midst of change and uncertainty.

5 THINGS TO PRAY

PRAYING WHEN WE ARE...

IN CONFLICT WITH ONE ANOTHER

EPHESIANS 4 v 25-32

PRAYER POINTS:

Father, if we have conflict with one another let us...

 SPEAK TRUTHFULLY

"Each of you must put off falsehood and speak truthfully" (v 25).

In every quarrel there is always the temptation to exaggerate the other person's sins and downplay our own. Pray that God would allow each of you to speak truthfully in the midst of conflict. Also, ask the Lord to give you the courage to speak the truth, even if it's difficult or awkward, knowing that it's better to be honest than to suppress the truth and let bitterness grow.

 RECONCILE QUICKLY

"Do not let the sun go down while you are still angry" (v 26).

When conflict is left unresolved sometimes it can become entrenched. As a result, some conflicts can last days, weeks, and even years. Pray that any conflict you face would be resolved as quickly as possible. Ask for grace to be the first to apologize, the first to forgive, and the first to move toward the other person.

PUT AWAY BITTERNESS

"Get rid of all bitterness" (v 31).

If conflict occurs over the course of many years, bitterness has a way of setting in. Spouses can begin to resent one another if they have been hurt over and over again. Pray that the Lord would prevent a root of bitterness from taking hold in your marriage. Ask the Lord to reveal in what ways you might need to apologize to your spouse for past wrongs.

 BE KIND

"Be kind ... to one another" (v 32).

Praise God today for his kindness to you—even though you did nothing to deserve it. Ask God to give you a heart that is tender and affectionate toward your spouse, demonstrated in simple acts of kindness toward them each day. Pray also that the Lord would show you tangible ways to do good to your spouse, even if they are not always good to you in return.

 FORGIVE ONE ANOTHER

"Forgiving each other, just as in Christ God forgave you" (v 32).

It's hard to truly forgive those who wrong us. Sometimes we may even want to withhold forgiveness. Rejoice that Christ forgave you when you were undeserving. Pray that God would give both you and your spouse a heart that recognizes how much you've been forgiven so that you can, in turn, freely and readily forgive one another.

5 THINGS TO PRAY

PRAYING WHEN WE ARE...

MAKING A DIFFICULT DECISION

ROMANS 12 v 1-2

PRAYER POINTS:

_____

_____

_____

_____

Father, as we make this decision, help us choose what is...

 SACRIFICIAL

> *"I urge you, brothers and sisters, in view of God's mercy, to offer your bodies as a living sacrifice" (v 1).*

Making decisions is difficult. It's tempting to seek the easiest, most comfortable solution. Yet, in view of God's mercy, we are called to present our bodies as living sacrifices, willing to follow our Savior in the way of the cross. Pray that the Lord would help you and your spouse to choose what is most honoring to his name, even when it comes at a cost.

 HOLY AND ACCEPTABLE

> *"... holy and pleasing to God" (v 1).*

Praise God that he is with you as you make this decision. He cares about your needs, and promises to guide you. Pray that the choice you make would be holy and pleasing in his sight. Ask God to allow you and your spouse to walk in a manner worthy of the gospel as you seek to follow him.

DIFFERENT FROM THE WORLD

"Do not conform to the pattern of this world" (v 2).

It's tempting to make decisions with the same priorities and motives as our non-Christian neighbors. Prayerfully bring the different elements of this decision before God, asking him to convict you of any worldly thinking by the power of his Spirit.

 ACCORDING TO YOUR WORD

"… but be transformed by the renewing of your mind" (v 2).

As we spend time in God's word, it changes us. While it may not speak directly to your specific situation, it will grow your discernment as it teaches you how to live. Prayerfully ask God to transform your minds and guide you together in what is right.

 DISCERNING

"Then you will be able to test and approve what God's will is—his good, pleasing, and perfect will" (v 2).

In marriage, it can be difficult when there is disunity or disagreement about a decision, particularly when it involves significant changes. It's good and wise to seek counsel from pastors, mentors, and friends to help guide you both. Pray that the Lord will give you spiritual discernment and unity in your marriage as you seek to do his will.

5 THINGS TO PRAY

PRAYING WHEN WE ARE...

SUFFERING ILLNESS

JAMES 5 v 13-16

PRAYER POINTS:

Father, in our physical ailments let us...

 NOT BE SURPRISED

"Is anyone among you in trouble?" (v 13).

When we suffer physical sickness, sometimes we are surprised. But in a fallen, broken world, such illnesses are to be expected. Pray that God would give you peace about your health, and that you would not fret, worry, or wonder, "Why me?" Pray instead that your illness would remind you why we need the Lord Jesus—to solve the curse of sin on the world.

 OFFER UP PRAYERS

"Let them pray" (v 13).

God is Lord over all of creation, including illnesses like cancer, diabetes, arthritis, and heart disease. He is the ultimate place you must turn, whatever illness you or your spouse are enduring. So come to your heavenly Father in prayer now, knowing that he hears you. Ask him to give you a deep trust in his power and compassion. Pray also that your illness would help you draw closer to God instead of drifting further away.

84

3 ASK FOR HELP

"Call the elders of the church" (v 14).

It's one thing to suffer an illness, it is another to suffer alone. Thank God that he has provided his body—the church—to be a source of comfort and help in times of physical need. Pray that God would use elders, pastors, and friends in your life to love you, pray for you, and care for you when you are suffering from illness. Also, ask the Lord to take away any pride or hesitancy that might keep you from asking for help.

4 TRUST THE LORD

"The Lord will raise them up" (v 15).

While help from doctors and friends is important, our greatest need is God's help. He is the one who ultimately heals our infirmities—so ask him to do that. And ask that, if God does not remove the illness, he would provide the grace to endure it until the day you are resurrected in glory.

5 CONFESS OUR SINS

"Confess your sins to each another ... that you may be healed" (v 16).

While not all illnesses are due to sin, some are (John 5 v 14). Thus, an important step in the healing process is to be willing to confess your sins. Ask God to show you and your spouse areas where you need to turn back to God and his ways. Pray that the Lord would give you the power to change, and that he would remind you that you are forgiven fully in Jesus Christ.

5 THINGS TO PRAY

PRAYING WHEN WE ARE...

RAISING CHILDREN

DEUTERONOMY 6 v 5-7

PRAYER POINTS:

_____

_____

_____

_____

Father, as we raise a family help us to...

 LOVE THE LORD

"Love the LORD your God" (v 5).

We can never teach our children what we don't know ourselves. If we want them to love the Lord, we need a deep affection for God ourselves. Pray that you and your spouse will love the Lord and hold fast to him all the days of your life.

 OBEY THE WORD

"... with all your heart and with all your soul and with all your strength" (v 5).

We want to show our children what it means to love the Lord with our affections *and* with our actions. If they hear us say, "Tell the truth" but then hear us tell a lie, our actions will speak louder than our words. Pray that your love for the Lord will be a life-consuming and life-changing example for your children, as you follow him with all of your heart, all of your soul, and with all of your might.

KNOW YOUR WORD

"These commandments that I give you today are to be on your hearts" (v 6).

Making time to read, study, and meditate on Scripture each day as parents will bless our children. In what ways does your heart particularly need to be changed by God's word with regards to your parenting? Pray for that now.

 TEACH YOUR WORD

"Impress them on your children" (v 7).

Pray that your time spent teaching your children about God would be full of wonder and delight, as you read colorful children's books about God, sing songs that help them memorize Scripture, or pray with them daily. Ask God to give you and your spouse wisdom, creativity, and diligence as you teach your children today.

 TALK ABOUT YOUR WORD

"Talk about them when you sit ... you walk ... you lie down ... you get up" (v 7).

Take some time today to thank God for the children he has given you—each child is a special blessing! Prayerfully ask God for special moments during your day to teach spiritual truths. Ask for opportunities as you ride in the car, share a meal, or play a game to teach God's word to your children. Pray that the Lord will give them eyes to see and ears to hear the good news of the gospel.

5 THINGS TO PRAY

PRAYING WHEN WE ARE...

CELEBRATING GOOD NEWS

PSALM 100

PRAYER POINTS:

Father, let us celebrate your great blessings with…

 JOY

"Shout for joy to the LORD, all the earth"
_(v 1)._

Praise God for his goodness to you! The lives of Christians should be marked by joy. Paul is very plain: "Rejoice always" (1 Thessalonians 5 v 16). Whenever you receive good news, no matter how small, ask the Lord to renew the joy in your hearts and to let it overflow into your lives.

 SONG

"Come before him with joyful songs" (v 2).

One of the most natural ways to offer worship to God is through the power of song. Again, Paul notes this should characterize our lives: "… speaking to one another with psalms, hymns, and songs from the Spirit" (Ephesians 5 v 19). So sing heartily to the Lord now in thanksgiving for the blessings he has given you. Pray that the Lord would use your singing to glorify his name and to lift up your spirits.

3 OTHERS

"Enter his gates ... and his courts with praise" (v 4).

Although we can worship God in private, it is most fitting to do so publicly as we "enter his gates" and gather together with God's people. Thank God for those who love you and who are rejoicing with you, and pray that the Lord would provide a deep, rich community of believers who can join you as you celebrate God's goodness in your life.

4 THANKSGIVING

"Give thanks to him" (v 4).

One of the signs that a person understands the mercy they have been shown is that they offer thanksgiving. So do that now! Pray that God would take away any ingratitude in your hearts and replace it with a new posture of gratitude for his goodness.

5 TRUTH

"For the LORD is good" (v 5).

We're not just called to delight in what God does but in what he is like. One of the main ways that we praise God is to make true declarations about him. It glorifies God when we affirm his character, his qualities, or his deeds. Take some time to think through all the wonderful character attributes of God (good, loving, merciful, etc.). Then say these attributes out loud as a declaration of praise to him.

EXPLORE THE WHOLE SERIES

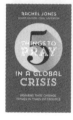  

"A THOUGHT-PROVOKING, VISION-EXPANDING, PRAYER-STIMULATING TOOL. SIMPLE, BUT BRILLIANT."

SINCLAIR FERGUSON

thegoodbook.com | .co.uk

thegoodbook
COMPANY

BIBLICAL | RELEVANT | ACCESSIBLE

At The Good Book Company, we are dedicated to helping Christians and local churches grow. We believe that God's growth process always starts with hearing clearly what he has said to us through his timeless word—the Bible.

Ever since we opened our doors in 1991, we have been striving to produce Bible-based resources that bring glory to God. We have grown to become an international provider of user-friendly resources to the Christian community, with believers of all backgrounds and denominations using our books, Bible studies, devotionals, evangelistic resources, and DVD-based courses.

We want to equip ordinary Christians to live for Christ day by day, and churches to grow in their knowledge of God, their love for one another, and the effectiveness of their outreach.

Call us for a discussion of your needs or visit one of our local websites for more information on the resources and services we provide.

Your friends at The Good Book Company

thegoodbook.com | thegoodbook.co.uk
thegoodbook.com.au | thegoodbook.co.nz
thegoodbook.co.in